Building Occult Character

By Annie Besant
C. W. Leadbeater

ISBN: 978-1-63118-626-4

Esoteric Classics

Other Books in this Series and Related Titles

Aurora of the Philosophers by Paracelsus (978-1-63118-507-6)

Rosicrucian Rules, Secret Signs, Codes and Symbols by various (978-1-63118-488-8)

On the Philadelphian Gold by Philochrysus & Philadelphus (978-1-63118-511-3)

Paracelsus, the Four Elements and Their Spirits by M P Hall (978-1-63118-400-0)

The Stone of the Philosophers by A E Waite (978-1-63118-509-0)

Clairvoyance and Psychic Abilities by A Besant &c (978-1-63118-403-1)

The Rosicrucian Chemical Marriage by Christian Rosenkreuz (978-1-63118-458-1)

The Alchemical Catechism of Paracelsus by Paracelsus (978-1-63118-513-7)

Alchemy in the Nineteenth Century by Helena P. Blavatsky (978-1-63118-446-8)

Rosicrucians and Speculative Masonry in the Seventeenth Century (978-1-63118-489-5)

Qabbalistic Teachings and the Tree of Life by M P Hall (978-1-63118-482-6)

The Sepher Yetzirah and the Qabalah by M P Hall (978-1-63118-481-9)

The Devil in Love by Jacques Cazotte (978–1–63118–499–4)

Fortune-Telling with Dice by Astra Cielo (978-1-63118-466-6)

History, Analysis and Secret Tradition of the Tarot by Hall &c (978-1-63118-445-1)

Crystal Vision Through Crystal Gazing by Frater Achad (978-1-63118-455-0)

The Golden Verses of Pythagoras: Five Translations (978-1-63118-479-6)

Arcane Formulas or Mental Alchemy by W W Atkinson (978-1-63118-459-8)

The Machinery of the Mind by Dion Fortune (978-1-63118-451-2)

The A E Waite Reader: A Selection of Occult Essays (978-1-63118-515-1)

The Leadbeater Reader: A Selection of Occult Essays (978-1-63118-483-3)

Audio versions are also available on Audible, Amazon and Apple

Other Books in this Series and Related Titles

The Book of the Nephilim by Enoch (978-1-63118-627-1)

Ancient Egyptian Mysteries and Hieroglyphics, Modern Freemasonry & Initiation of the Pyramid (978-1-63118-625-7) HC

The Lost Book of Noah by Noah (978-1-63118-624-0)

The Acts of Saint Andrew by Andrew (978-1-63118-623-3)

The Acts of the Apostle John by John (978–1–63118–622–6)

Karmic Visions by Helena P. Blavatsky (978–1–63118–621–9)

The Ascension of Isaiah by Isaiah (978-1-63118-620-2)

The Mysteries of Mithra by G R S Mead (978-1-63118-619-6)

Second Book of Enoch by Enoch (978-1-63118-617-2)

Lost Keys of Freemasonry by Manly P Hall (978-1-63118-616-5)

Book of the Watchers by Enoch (978-1-63118-615-8)

Sepher Yetzirah and the Qabalah by Manly P Hall (978-1-63118-614-1)

Philosophy of Self-Knowledge by Franz Hartmann (978-1-63118-613-4)

Occult Symbolism of the Sun and Moon, the Goddess Isis and thee Solar Deities by Manly P Hall (978–1–63118–611–0)

Practical Theosophy by Annie Besant (978–1–63118–610–3)

The Human Body in Symbolism by Manly P Hall (978–1–63118–609–7)

Theosophical Basics by William Q Judge (978–1–63118–608–0)

The Hebrew Talisman by Richard Harte (978–1–63118–607–3)

Early Masonic Symbolism by Manly P Hall (978–1–63118–606–6)

Nature Spirits and Elementals by Louise Off (978-1-63118-605-9)

Audio versions are also available on Audible, Amazon and Apple

Table of Contents

Introduction

The word "esoteric" can be difficult to define. Esotericism in general can be seen less as a system of beliefs and more as a category, which encompasses numerous, different systems of beliefs. It's a bit of juxtaposition, since the word "esoteric" indicates something that few people know about, while the term itself broadly covers numerous philosophies, practices, areas of study and belief systems.

In a greater sense, Esotericism acts as a storehouse for secret knowledge, which is often considered ancient (by *tradition, if not by fact),* passed down from generation to generation, in private. At various times in history, simply possessing the knowledge of some of these subjects, was considered illegal and a jailable offence, if discovered. This usually included such general topics as Alchemy, Qabalah, Hermeticism, Occultism, Ceremonial Magic, Astrology, Divination, Rosicrucianism and so on. Collectively, these areas of study were often referred to as the esoteric sciences.

Sometimes, the outer garment of a subject isn't esoteric, while what is hidden beneath it, is. As an example, Freemasonry isn't necessarily esoteric by nature (at *least not anymore),* but certain signs, passwords and handshakes given to the candidate during their initiation, are in fact, esoteric, in the sense that they are hidden from the general public.

Today, in the twenty-first century, such topics are readily available at bookstores across the country, and numerous mainsteam publishers offer beginners guides and coffee-table volumes on many of these subjects, intended for mass appeal. Books like "*The Secret*" have turned previously arcane topics into household knowledge. All that being the case, however, it isn't to say that there still aren't buried secrets to uncover, ancient wisdom being ignored and forgotten mysteries to be explored. In fact, it is often that we are only able to further our own studies by standing on the shoulders of these disappearing giants.

Lamp of Trismegistus is doing its part to help preserve humanity's esoteric history by making some of these classics available to those students who are seeking to unearth the knowledge of these ancient colossi.

So, be sure to check other titles from our *Esoteric Classics* series, as well as our *Occult Fiction*, *Theosophical Classics*, *Foundations of Freemasonry* and our *Christian Apocrypha Series.* You can also download the audio versions of most of these titles from iTunes or Audible.

THE BUILDING OF CHARACTER

Annie Besant

IN beginning this lecture, I want as a preliminary step to warn you with regard to the qualifications with which I am dealing, and the line of thought and of action which will be followed by those who are in the mystical position that I call "In the Outer Court". The position of an aspirant who had reached that Court is very different from the position even of the good and virtuous and religious man, who has not thoroughly seen the goal which is before him, who has not thoroughly realized the magnitude of his task. And I want to remind you that in the whole of this in which I am sketching the qualifications of those who come into the Court, I am dealing with everything from this standpoint of a deliberate self-training towards an aim that is definitely recognized; and more than that, that I by no means mean in speaking of these qualifications that they are completely achieved while the aspirant still remains in the Outer Court of the Temple. He begins, as it were, the making of the character, he realizes to some extent what he ought to be, and he strives more or less effectively to become that which he aspires to achieve. It is not that the definite purification, or the complete control of the thoughts, or the perfect building of the character, or the entire transmutation of the lower into the higher — it is not that all these must be accomplished ere he can stand on the threshold of the Temple; he is really employed whilst in the Outer Court in drawing as it were the foundations of his buildings, in sketching out carefully and fairly fully the outlines of that edifice which he hopes to carry to perfection. The working out of all these lines, the building on this foundation, the raising of the walls higher and higher, the placing of the crowning stone finally upon the work — that is done rather within the Temple than without it, after the eyes have been opened, not while they are still partially blinded and the aspirant is in the Outer Court. But what I do want you to understand is that the plan is sketched, that the plan is recognized; that nothing less than this — very much more may come in the course of the ages — that nothing less than this is the goal that the candidate sets before himself for the reaching; so that however great may seem the aspirations, however magnificent may seem the outline which is to be filled in, that outline is to be definitely recognized in the Outer Court, although not to be filled in in detail, and however lowly may be the achievements of the present they are none the less the definite foundations on which the glorious achievements of the future are to be based. And I say this thus explicitly, although it be a repetition, because it was suggested to me that in making so wide a scope for the Outer Court, in tracing so vast an outline, it might come on some of my hearers with a sense of discouragement if not of despair; so that it is well that all should understand that while the beginnings are traced they may still be only the beginnings, and that after the threshold is crossed, there are still many lives in front in which these beginnings may be carried to fulfillment, and this plan of the architect serves as basis for the finished edifice. Taking then that as a thing to be understood, let me remind you of the building of the character, which is to be a distinct and a positive building which this candidate in the Outer Court will set before himself; we have seen already that he is to have been in past lives a virtuous and a religious man, that is, that he will have already realized that nothing of absolute vice must have its place in him, that nothing of evil must be permitted to remain; that if any seed of vice remain, it, must at once be flung without, that if any tendencies towards positive evil are still there, they must be completely and entirely rooted out. Here in this Court there can be at least no compromise with evil, here there can be at least no paltering with that which is not right and pure and good. While there may still be failures in the achievement of the right, there is most definitely no contented remaining in the wrong; that has had the back of the aspirant definitely turned upon it, and all the grosser part of the nature will already have been eliminated, all the rougher part of the inner struggle will have been finished. Into the Court of the Temple utterly unhewn stones cannot be brought for the building; the hewing must have been going on during many previous lives, much work must have been done upon the characters before they become fit to be built at all even in the Outer Court of such a Temple. And this rough-hewing of the character is supposed to lie behind us; we are dealing with the building of the positive virtues, and virtues of an exceedingly high and noble type;

virtues which are not those simply that are recognized as necessary in the world, but far rather those which the aspirant desires to achieve in order that he may become one of the Helpers and the Saviours of the world, those characteristics that go to make up one of the world's Redeemers, one of the pioneers of the first-fruits of mankind.

The first thing perhaps that will strike us, in this building of character by one who is in the Outer Court, is its exceedingly deliberate nature. It is not a thing of fits and starts, it is not a casual building and leaving off, it is not an effort in this direction one day and in another direction tomorrow, it is not a running about seeking for aims, it is not a turning about looking for a purpose; the whole of this at least is definitely done, the purpose is recognized and the aim is known. And the building is a deliberate building, as by one who knows that he has time, and that nothing in Nature can be lost; a deliberate building which begins with the materials ready to hand, which begins with the character as it is recognized to exist, which looks, as we shall see, quietly at all its strength and at all its weaknesses, and sets to work to improve the one and to remedy the other; a deliberate building towards a definite aim, a carving in permanent material of a statue of which the mould has already been made.

And so the first thing that will be noticed in these candidates in the Outer Court is this definiteness of purpose and this deliberateness of action. The man knows that he will carry everything on that he makes; that from life to life he will take with him the treasures that he has accumulated; that if he finds a deficiency and only partly fills it up, still it is filled up to that extent, that part of the work is done; that if he makes for himself a power, that power is his for evermore, a part of the Soul never to be taken away from it, woven into the texture of the individual, not again ever to be separated from him. And he builds with this deliberate purpose which has its root in knowledge, recognizing the Law that underlies every aspect of Nature. Realizing that that Law is changeless, knowing that he may trust it with uttermost and completest faith, he calls upon the Law and knows that the Law will answer, he appeals to the Law and is confident that the Law will judge. There is in him then no trace of wavering, no shadow of doubting; he gives out that which must needs bring to him his harvest, and every seed that he sows, he sows with this absolute certainty that the seed will bear fruit after its kind, that that and none other will come back to him in future days. So there is naught of hurry in his work, naught of impatience in his labour; if the fruit be not ripe, he can wait for the gathering; if the seed be not ready, he can wait for the growing. He knows that this Law to which he has given himself is at once changeless and good; that the Law will bring all in its appointed time, and that the appointed time is best for him and for the world. And so, as I said, he starts with his available material, content with it because it is what the Law brings him from his past; content with it, because it is that with which he has to work, that and nothing else; and whether full or scanty, whether poor and small or rich and great, he takes it and begins to work with it, knowing that however scanty it be there is no limit to the wealth to which it may be increased, and knowing that however small it may bulk today, there is no limit to the vastness to which it may grow in the years which lie in front. He knows that he must succeed; not a question of possibility but of certitude, not a question of chance but of definite reality. The Law must give back the equivalent of that which he gives, and even if he give but little, that little will come back to him, and from that he will build in the future, adding always something to the store, standing a little higher with each achievement, with each new accomplishment.

Already we know something of the way in which he will build; we know that he will begin with right thought. Elsewhere [*A Study in Consciousness, by Annie Besant or Thought Power: Its Control and Culture, by Annie Besant*] we have studied this control of the thoughts, which is necessary in order that the right may be chosen, and the wrong may be rejected. Working steadily at that thought-control and knowing its conditions, understanding the laws, by which thoughts are generated and by which thoughts act in the world and react upon their generator, he is now in a condition definitely to choose right thought for the building of his character. And this stage of right thinking will be one of the early steps that he will take while he is traversing the Outer Court. First of all because his right thinking affects others — and all those who are thus candidates for the Temple have their primary motive in the service of others — so that, in the choosing of his thought, in the selection of the thoughts that he either generates or permits to come within his consciousness, his first motive for such choice will be the effect that these thoughts will have upon others, not in the first place the effect they will have upon himself; for above and beyond all else he is qualifying for service, and therefore as he chooses the thoughts to which he will bend his energy, he calculates their action on the outer world — how far they will work for helping, how far they will work for strengthening, how far they will work for purifying; and into the great stream of thoughts that he knows must go out from his consciousness, understanding how that stream is working, he will send the thoughts that are useful to others, with the deliberate purpose of this serving, with the deliberate object of this helping of the world.

And next he will consider the nature of the thoughts as they affect himself, as they react upon him to make his character, a thing that in a few moments we shall see is of the most vital importance, for here indeed is the instrument by which the character will be built; and not only as they react upon his character, but also as, in making that character, they turn it into a magnet for other thoughts, so that he, acting as a focus for high and noble thoughts — not now, we may hope, for thoughts that are actively injurious — will deliberately make his consciousness a magnet for everything that is good, so that all that is evil may die as it strikes against him, and all that is good may flow into his consciousness to gain there fresh nourishment, to gain there fresh strength and fresh energy; that the good thoughts of others coming to him may go out with new life-impulse given to them, and that he may act not only as a source of help by the thoughts he generates, but as a channel of helping by the thoughts that he receives, that he revivifies, and that he transmits. And these will go to the making of character, so that at the beginning of the building this right thinking will be one dominant influence in his mind, and he will constantly be watching his thoughts, scrutinizing them with the most jealous care, in order that into this sanctuary of the consciousness nothing may come which will offend, for unless this be guarded all else is left open to the enemy. It is the very citadel of the castle; at the same time it is the gateway through which everything enters in.

And then he will learn in this building of character — perhaps he has already learned — to guard his speech; for right speech, to begin with, must be true, scrupulously and accurately true, not with the commonplace truthfulness of the world, though that be not a thing to be despised, but of that scrupulous and strict truthfulness which is necessary above all to the student of Occultism — truth of observation, truth of recording, truth of thinking, truth of speaking, truth of acting; for where there is not this seeking after truth and this strenuous determination to become true, there is no possibility of Occultism which is aught but a danger, there is no possibility of anything but fall, deep and terrible, in proportion to the height to which the student may have climbed. For this quality of truth in the Occultist is at once his guide and his shield: his guide, in that it gives him the insight which enables him to choose the true road from the false, the right hand path from the left; and his shield, in that only as he is covered with this shield of truth, can all the delusions and the glamours of the planes through which he passes fall harmless. For it is in the practice of truth in thought, in speech, and in act, that there gradually wakes up that spiritual insight which pierces through every veil of illusion, and against which there can be in Nature no possibility of setting up a successful deception. Everywhere veils are spread, everywhere in the world of illusion this deceitfulness of appearances is to be found, until the spiritual insight can pierce through the whole of them with unchanging and direct vision. There is no such thing as the development of spiritual insight, save as truth is followed in the character, as truth is cultivated in the intellect, as truth is developed in the conscience; without this nothing, but failure, without this nothing but inevitable blunder and mistake.

The speech first of all, then, will be true, and next it will be gentle. For truth and gentleness are not in opposition, as too often we are inclined to think, and speech loses nothing of its truth by being perfect in its gentleness and perfect also in its courtesy and its compassion. The more true it is the more gentle it needs must be, for at the very heart of all things is truth and also compassion; therefore the speech that reflects the innermost essence of the Universe can neither causelessly wound any living being, nor be false with the slightest shadow of suspicion. True and gentle then the speech must be, true and gentle and courteous; that is said to be the austerity of speech, the true penance and sacrifice of speech which is offered up by every aspirant. And then out of the right speaking and the right thinking, inevitably must flow right acting; that, as an outcome, must be the result of this flowing forth from the source. For action is only the manifestation of that which is within, and where the thought is pure, where the speech is true and right, there the action must inevitably be noble; out of such sweet source the water can only be sweet in the flowing, out of the heart and the brain that have been purified necessarily the action must be right and good. And that is the threefold cord by which the aspirant is bound alike to humanity and to his Master; the threefold cord which, in some great religions, stands as type of this perfect self-control; self-control in thought, in speech and in action — that is the triple cord which binds the man to service that is perfect in its character, which binds the disciple to the feet of his Master; the threefold cord which may not easily be broken.

When all this is realized, and the beginning of it attempted, this candidate of ours will begin a very definite method of practice in his building of the character, and first he will form what is called an "Ideal". Let us have clearly in the mind what we mean when we use this word "Ideal". The mind working within itself builds an internal image, which is made as the mind grows in strength out of much that it draws from the outer world; but although it draws the materials from the outer world, the idea is the result of the internal action of the mind upon the materials. An idea is at its highest an abstract thing, and if we realize how the abstract idea is formed in the mere brain-consciousness, we shall then have a very clear view of what is meant by an ideal; a little enlargement of the idea will give us exactly what we require. Let me take the ancient illustration, an abstract idea of a triangle. The idea of a triangle may be gained at first by the brain-consciousness working in the child through a study of many forms which he is told are triangles. He will notice that they are of many different shapes, that they are made up of lines which go in very different directions. He will find — when he looks at them separately and with this brain-consciousness of the child — he will find them exceedingly different, so that looking at them at first he will see them as many figures, and will not recognize certain underlying unities which give them all the same name. But as he goes onward in his thinking he will gradually learn that there are certain definite conceptions which underlie this one conception of the triangle; that it always has three lines and no more; that it always has three angles and no more; that these three angles put together have always a certain definite value, and that the three lines, called the sides of the triangle, bear certain relations to each other, and so on. All these different conceptions he will gain as he studies, and the mind, working upon the whole of these, extracts from them what is called an abstract idea of a triangle, which has no particular size, and no particular shape, and no particular angles taken separately. And this abstract idea is made up by the working of the mind on all the many concrete forms, so far as the brain-consciousness is concerned. What greater idea this may be the reflection of, I am not now considering; but it is thus that in the brain what is called an abstract idea is built, which has neither colour nor shape nor any special characteristic of any one form, and which unites within itself that which makes the many forms of it a unity. And so when we build an ideal it is an idea of this abstract kind, it is the work of the image-building faculty of the mind, which draws out the essence of all the different ideas that it has gained of great virtues — of that which is beautiful, of that which is true, of that which is harmonious, of that which is compassionate, of that which is in every sense satisfying to the aspirations of the mind, of the heart. From all these different ideas, as they have been seen limited in manifestation, the essence is extracted, and then the mind constructs and throws outwards a vast heroic figure in which everything is carried to perfection; in which everything touches its highest and most complete expression; in which we no longer deal with the things that are true, but with truth; no longer with the things that are beautiful, but with beauty; no longer with the things that are strong, but with strength; no longer with the things that are tender, but with tenderness; no longer with the beings who are loving, but with love; and this perfect figure — mighty and harmonious in all its proportions, grander than anything we have seen, only not grander than that which in rare moments of inspiration the Spirit has cast downwards into the mind — that ideal of perfection it is which the aspirant makes for himself as perfect as he is able to conceive it, knowing all the time that his most perfect dreaming is but the faintest shadow of the reality whence this reflection has come. For in the world of the Real, there exists in living light that which down here he sees, as it were, in faint reflection of colour, hanging high in the heavens over the snowy mountains of human aspiration; it is still only the shadow of the Reality whence it has been reflected, all that the human soul may image of the perfect, of the sublime, of the ultimate All that we seek. This ideal he forms is still imperfect, for it must needs be so! But, however imperfect it may be, none the less for him it is the ideal according to which his character is to be built.

But why make an ideal? Those of you who have gone so far with me in the working of thought will know why an ideal is necessary. Let me take two sentences, one from a great Hindu Scripture and the other from a Christian, to show you how Initiates speak of the same facts, no matter in what tongue they talk, no matter to what civilization their words may be addressed. It is written in one of the most mystical of the Upanishads, the Chhãndogya: "Man is a creature of reflection; what he reflects upon, that he becomes; therefore reflect upon Brahman." And many thousand years afterwards another great Teacher, one of the builders of Christianity, wrote exactly the same thought put into other words: "But we all, with open face beholding as in a glass the glory of the Lord, are changed into the same image from glory to glory." Beholding as in a glass: for the mind is a mirror and images are cast upon it and are reflected, and the Soul that in the mirror of the mind beholds the glory of the Lord is changed into that same image from glory to glory. So that whether you take the Hindu speaker or the Christian, whether you read the scripture of the Indian or the scripture of the Western Sage, still the same teaching of the Brotherhood comes out to you — that you must have the ideal before you in order that you may reflect it, and that that on which the mind is constantly dwelling will inevitably be that which the man shall become.

And how shall the building towards the ideal be made? For that is the question that we must now consider. By contemplation: definitely, with full purpose, choosing his time and not permitting himself to be shaken from it, this aspirant who is disciplining his own character will contemplate day by day the ideal that he has built. He will fix his mind upon it, and constantly reflect it in his consciousness. Day by day he will go over its outline, day by day he will dwell upon it in thought, and, as he contemplates, inevitably within him will rise up that reverence and that awe which are worship, the great transforming power by which the man becomes that which he adores, and this contemplation will essentially be the contemplation of reverence and of aspiration. And as he contemplates, the rays of the Divine Ideal will shine down upon him, and the aspiration upwards will open the windows of the Soul to receive them; so that they shall illuminate him from within, and then cast a light without, the ideal shining ever above and within him, and marking out the path along which his feet must tread. And in order that he may thus contemplate, he must train himself in concentration; the mind is not to be scattered, as our minds so often are. We have to learn to fix it, and to fix it steadily, and this is a thing that we should be working at continually, working at in all the common things of life, doing one thing at a time until the mind answers obediently to the impulse, and doing it with the concentrated energy which bends the whole mind towards a single point. No matter that many things that you have to do are trivial; it is the way of doing them, and not the things that are done, that makes the training which results in discipleship — not the particular kind of work that you have to do in the world, but the way that you do it, the mind that you bring to it, the forces with which you execute it, the training that you gain from it. And it matters not what the life may be, that life will serve for the purpose of the training; for however trivial may be the particular work in which you are engaged at the moment, you can use it as a training-ground for the mind, and by your concentration you may be making your mind one-pointed, no matter what for the moment may be the point to which it is directed. For remember, when once you have gained the faculty, then you can choose the object; when once the mind is definitely in your hand, so that you can turn it hither and thither as you will, then you can choose for yourself the end to which it shall be directed. But you may just as well practise and gain the control in little things as in great; in fact, very much better, because the little things are around us every day, whereas the great things come but seldom. When the great thing comes, the whole mind arouses itself to meet it; when the great thing comes, the whole attention is fixed upon it; when the great thing comes, every energy is called to play upon it, so that you may bear yourself well when the mighty task is to be accomplished. But the real value of the Soul is tested more in the little things where there is nothing to arouse attention, nothing in any sense to gain applause, where the man is deliberately working for the end that he has chosen, and is using everything around him in order that he may discipline himself. That self-discipline is the key of the whole. Guide your life by some plan; make to yourself certain rules into which your life shall flow; and when you have made them, keep to them, and alter them only as deliberately as at first you formed them. Take so simple a thing — for the body has to be brought under control — take so simple a thing as a definite rule of rising in the morning; fix the time that you feel is best for your work, for your place in your household, and when you have fixed it, keep to it. Do not permit the body at the moment to choose its own time, but train it in that instant and automatic obedience which makes it a useful servant of the mind. And if you find after practising for some time that you have chosen badly, then change; do not be rigid because you are striving to strengthen your will; be ready to change what does not work well; but change it at your own time and with perfect deliberation; do not change it because on the impulse of the moment passion or bodily desire or emotion may be ruling; do not change it at the demand of the lower nature that has to be disciplined, but change it if you find that you have badly chosen. For never in ruling your own life must you make your rule a hindrance to those around you, or choose ways of self-discipline that aggravate or interrupt others instead of simply training yourself.

The next stage, when all this has been clearly recognized as the way in which the character is to be built, will be to study the character itself; for you are to work with knowledge and not blindly. You will perhaps, if you are wise, in judging your character, take some of the things that great men have put before you as outlining a character which will lead you to the Gate of the Temple. You might take, for instance, such a tracing as is given in the sixteenth discourse in the Bhagavad-Gita, by Sri Krishna to Arjuna, where he is telling Arjuna what should be the qualities which build up the divine character. You might take that as showing you the qualities at which you should aim in building yourself, and as marking out for you that which you desire gradually to evolve. And if you take it as it is sketched in the sixteenth discourse, you find a list of qualities, every one of which might well serve as part of your constant thought and endeavour, remembering that the character is built first by the contemplation of the virtue, and then by the working out of that virtue which has become part of the thought into the speech and the action in daily life. And the list runs — however great it is, we have time enough before us to fill it in — "Fear-lessness, Purity of Heart, Steadfastness in the Yoga of Wisdom, Almsgiving, Self-restraint and Sacrifice, and Study of the Sastras, Austerity and Straightforwardness, Harmlessness, Truth, Absence of Wrath, Renunciation, Peacefulness, Absence of Calumny, Compassion to Living Beings, Uncovetousness, Mildness, Modesty, Absence of Fickleness, Boldness, Forgiveness, Fortitude, Uprightness, Amity, Absence of Pride — these become his who is born with the divine qualities." Not all are his at once, but become his, and are made in the building of the character. And you will find, if you read these at your leisure and with care, that you can group them together under very definite heads, and that each of these may be practised, at first of course very imperfectly but still steadily, and day by day — with never a feeling of discouragement at the lack of achievement, but only with joy in recognition of the goal, and knowing that each step is the step towards an end which shall be achieved. And notice how through them run the golden threads of unselfishness, of love, of harmlessness; see how courage and strength and endurance find also their place, so that you get an exquisite balance of character, a character that is at once strong and tender, that is at once self-reliant and compassionate, that is at once a helper of the weak and in itself strong and unmoved, that is full of devotion and full of harmlessness, that is full of self-discipline and therefore of harmony. Let us suppose you accept that to some extent as ideal for the guidance of daily thinking, and you begin to work it out; let us consider a point that is often found in connection with this effort, which is often found in summing up many virtues together, and which is much misunderstood; pausing a moment upon it, let us see how the building of character towards this virtue will be carried on. It is a name which is strange in English ears: it is indifference; and sometimes it is worked out in detail as indifference to pleasure and pain, indifference to cold and heat, indifference to blame and applause, indifference to desire and aversion, and so on; what does it really mean?

First of all, it means that sense of proportion which must come into the life of one who has gained a glimpse of the Real amid the fleeting, of the permanent amid the transitory; for when once the greatness of the goal has been recognized, when once the numberless lives have been realized, when once the aspirant has understood all the length of time that lies in front of him, all the vastness of the task that he is going to achieve, all the grandeur of the possibilities that lie still unveiled before him; when he has caught some glimpse of the Real, then all the things of one fleeting life must take their place in proportion to the whole. And when a trouble comes, that trouble will no longer bulk so largely as it did when one life was all that he realized, for he will begin to understand that he has been through many troubles before, and has come out the stronger and the more peaceful for the passage. And when joy comes, he will know that he has been through many joys before, and has learned their lessons also, and has found amid other things that they are transitory and so when a joy comes or a pain, he will take it, not failing to feel it, feeling it really far more keenly than the ordinary man of the world can feel, but feeling it in its true place and at its true worth, and giving it only its real value in the great scheme of life. So that as he grows in this indifference, it is not that he becomes less capable of feeling, for he is ever becoming more sensitive to every thrill of the world within and of the world without — inasmuch as he has become more harmonious with the All, he must become more responsive to every shade of harmony that is therein — but that none of these may avail to shake him, that none of these may avail to change him, that none of these may touch his serenity, that none of these may cast a shadow on his calm. For he himself is rooted where storms are not, he himself is grounded where changes have no place, and while he may feel, he can never be altered by them; they take their right place in life, they bear their proper proportion to the whole span of existence of the Soul. That indifference, that true and real indifference which means strength, how shall that develop?

First, by this daily thinking on what it means, and working it out bit by bit until you thoroughly understand it, and working out detail after detail, so that you know exactly what you mean by it. And then when you go out into the world of men, by practising it in your daily life; practising, not by hardening yourself but by making yourself responsive, not by making round yourself a shell that throws everything off, but by making yourself answer to everything that comes from without; at the same time keeping an inner balance which refuses to vary while the change is felt right through. A hard and a difficult lesson, but a lesson that has so much in it of hope and of joy and of keener and more vivid life, that if that were all it were worth while to practise it. For, as the Soul feels itself growing too strong to be shaken, and yet feels every thrill that comes from without, it has a sense of wider life, it has a sense of fuller harmony, it has a sense of ever-increasing consciousness, of ever-growing oneness with that of which it is part. And as the feeling of isolation gradually melts away there flows into it the joy which dwells at the heart of things, and even that which to the ordinary man is painful loses to the disciple its quality of pain; for he feels it, as it were, as part of the Universal Life, as a syllable which is spoken out of this vast language of Manifestation, and he can learn its meaning without any agony at his own heart, for the peace which grows out of this widening knowledge far overbears to him, and changes, as it were, his attitude towards everything in the outer world which men know as pain and loss. Thus thinking and thus practising, you will find this sense grow within you, this sense of calm and of strength and of serenity, so that you will feel as though you were in a place of peace, no matter what the storm in the outer world, and you will see and feel the storm and yet not be shaken by it. This peace is the first-fruits of the Spiritual Life, which shows itself first in this sense of peace and then in that of joy, and makes the life of the disciple a growth which is ever upwards and inwards to the heart which is Love. And out of this there grows the sense of self-control, that the Self within is stronger than the changes without, and while it is willing to respond, it refuses to be altered by the contacts from without. And then from the self-control and from the indifference there comes that power of hating none, on which so much stress is laid in all the building of character laid down for the aspirant who would become the disciple. Nothing is to be hated, everything is to be brought within the circle of Love, no matter how outwardly repulsive, no matter how outwardly antagonistic, no matter how outwardly repugnant; the heart of all is Life and Love, and therefore this aspirant who is learning his lessons can shut nothing out from the circle of compassion; everything is taken within it according to its own power of feeling, and he is the friend of every living thing, the lover of all that lives and feels.

And as he is thus building these stones into his character he becomes fearless; fearless, because hating nothing there is nothing that has power to harm. Injury from without is but the reaction of aggression from within; because we are the enemies of others they in their turn are our enemies, and because we go out into the world as injurers, therefore living things injure us in turn. We, who ought to be the lovers of all living things, go out as destroyers, as tyrants, as haters, grasping the world for tyranny and not for education, as though man's work here were not to educate his younger brethren and lead them upwards by all tenderness and all compassion; we go out and we tyrannize over others, whether they be human or brute, so long as they are weaker than ourselves; and by their weakness we too often measure our tyranny, and by their helplessness too often the burden that we lay upon them. And then we wonder that living things fly from us — that as we go out into the world we are met with dread from the weak, and with hatred from the strong; and we know not in our blindness that all the hatred from the outer world is the reflection of the evil that is in ourselves, and that to the heart of love there is nothing that is hateful, and therefore nothing that can injure. The man that has love can walk unharmed through the jungle, can walk untouched through the cave of the carnivorous brute, or take in his hands the serpent; for there is nothing that has message of hate to the heart that has in it only love, and the love that radiates to the world around us, that draws all things in to serve and not to injure, draws all things in to love and not to hate. And so at the feet of the Yogi the tiger will roll in friendship, and so to the feet of the saint the wildest will bring their young for shelter and for helping, and all living things will come to the man who loves, for they are all the offspring of the Divine, and the Divine is Love, and when that is made perfect in man it draws all things inwards to itself. So then we learn gradually and slowly to walk fearlessly in the world, fearlessly even though things may still injure; for we know if we are hurt that we are only paying the debt of an evil past, and that for every debt that is paid there is less against us, as it were, in the credit book of Nature. And fearless too, because we learn to know, and fear springs from doubt as well as from hatred; the man who knows has passed beyond doubt, and walks with foot unfearing where it may tread, for it treads on solid ground alone, and there are no pitfalls in its way. And out of this grows a firm and unshaken will, a will that is based on knowledge, and a will that grows confident through love. And as the aspirant is crossing the Court of the Outer Temple, his step becomes firmer, and his course becomes more direct, unshaken in its purpose and growing in its strength; his character begins to show itself out in definite outline, clear, distinct, and firm, the Soul growing onwards to maturity.

And then comes the absence of desire, the gradual getting rid of all those desires that tie us to the lower world, the gradual working out of all those longings which in the lives that lie behind us we found had no satisfaction for the Soul, the gradual casting aside of all the fetters that tie us down to earth, the gradual elimination of the personal desire, and the self-identification with the whole. For this one who is growing is not going to be tied to rebirth by any bonds that belong to the earth; men come back to the earth because they are held there, tied by these links of desire that bind them to the wheel of births and of deaths; but this man we are studying is going to be free; this man who is going to be free must break these links of desire for himself; there is only one thing that will bind him, only one thing that will draw him back to birth, and that is the love of his fellows, the desire of service. He is not bound to the wheel, for he is free, but he may come back and turn the wheel once more for the sake of those who still are bound upon it, and whom he will stand beside until the bonds of all Souls are broken. In his freeing he breaks the bonds of compulsion, and so he learns a perfect unselfishness, learns that what is good for all is that which he is seeking, and that what serves the All is that which alone he desires to achieve. And then he learns self-reliance; this one who is growing towards the Light, learns to be strong in order that he may help, learns to rely upon the Self which is the Self of all, with which he is growing to identify himself.

There is a thing that he has to face, upon which I must say a word, for it is perchance one of the hardest of his trials while he is working in this Outer Court. When he entered that Court, knowing and seeing the mighty joy beyond, he turned his back on much that makes life glad to his fellows; but there is a time that comes sometimes, there is a time that now and then descends upon the Soul, when, as it were, he has sprung outwards into a void where no hand seems to grasp his own, and where there is darkness around him, and nothing on which his feet may rest. There are times which come in these stages of the Soul's growth when there is nothing left on earth which can satisfy, there is nothing left on earth which can fill, when the friendships of old have lost some of their touch, and the delights of earth have lost all their savour, when the hands in front, though they are holding us, are not yet felt, when the rock beneath our feet, though our feet are planted upon it, is not yet understood as changeless and immovable, when by the veil of illusion the Soul is covered thickly, and it thinks itself forsaken and knows nothing of help that it can find. It is the void into which every aspirant in turn has plunged; it is the void that every disciple has crossed. When it yawns before the Soul, the Soul draws back; when it opens up dark and seemingly bottomless, he who stands upon the brink shrinks back in fear; and yet he need not fear. Plunge onwards into the void, and you shall find it full! Spring forward into the darkness and you shall find a rock beneath your feet! Let go the hands that hold you back, and mightier Hands in front will clasp your own and draw you onwards, and they are Hands that will never leave you. The earthly grasp will sometimes loosen, the friend's hand will unclasp your own and leave it empty, but the Friends who are on the other side never let go, no matter how the world may change. Go out then boldly into the darkness and into the loneliness, and you shall find the loneliness is the uttermost of delusions, and the darkness is a light which none may lose again in life. That trial, once faced, is found again to be a great delusion; and the disciple who dares to plunge finds himself on the other side.

Thus the building of character goes on, and will go on for lives to come, nobler and nobler as each life is ended, mightier and mightier as each step is taken. These foundations which we have been laying are only the foundations of the building I have hinted at, and if the achievement seem mighty, it is because always in the mind of the architect the building is complete, and even when the ground plan is a-sketching, his imagination sees the completed edifice, and he knows whereto he builds.

And the end ? Ah! — the ending of that building of character our tongues not yet can sketch! No paint-brush which is dipped only in earth's dull colours can limn anything of the beauty of that perfect ideal towards which we hope to, nay, towards which we know we shall, eventually rise. Have you ever caught a glimpse of it in silent moments ? Have you ever seen a reflection of it when the earth was still and when the heaven was calm ? Have you ever had a glimpse of those Divine Faces that live and move — Those that were men and now are more than men, superhuman in Their grandeur; man as he shall be though not as he is, save in the innermost Courts of the Temple? If you have ever caught a glimpse in your stillest moments, then you need no words of mine to tell you; you know of the compassion which at first seems the whole of the being, so radiant in its perfection, so glorious in its divinity; the tenderness which is so mighty that it can stoop to the lowest as well as transcend the highest, which recognizes the feeblest effort, as well as the mightiest achievement; nay, which is tenderer to the feeble than to the mighty, because the feeble most needs the helping of the sympathy which never changes the love which only seems not to be divine because it is so absolutely human, and in which we realize that man and God are one. And then beyond the tenderness, the strength — the strength that nothing can change, the strength which has in it the quality of the foundations of the Universe, on which all worlds might build, and yet it would not shake, strength so infinite joined with compassion so boundless. How can these qualities be in one Being and harmonize with such absolute perfection? And then the radiance of the joy — the joy that has conquered, the joy that would have all others share its beatitude, the radiant sunshine that knows no shadow, the glory of the conquest which tells that all shall win, the joy in the eyes that see beyond the sorrow, and that even in looking at pain know that the end is peace. Tenderness and strength and joy and uttermost peace — peace without a ruffle, serenity that naught can touch: such is the glimpse which you may have caught of the Divine, such is the glimpse of the ideal that one day we shall become. And if we dare to raise our eyes so high, it is because Their feet still tread the earth where our feet are treading. They have risen high above us; none the less stand They beside Their brothers, and if They transcend us it is not that They have left us, although on every side They are beyond us; for all humanity dwells in the heart of the Master, and where humanity is, we, its children, may dare to realize we dwell.

HOW TO BUILD CHARACTER

C. W. Leadbeater

THE very idea implied in the building of character is a new one to many people. They usually think and speak of a man as born with a certain character and practically incapable of changing it. They sometimes think of a man's character having been altered by great sorrow or suffering, as in truth it often is; but comparatively few people seem to realize that it is a thing that they can take in hand and mould for themselves — a thing at which they can steadily work with the certainty of obtaining good results. Yet it is true that a man may change himself intelligently and voluntarily, and may make of himself practically what he will within very wide limits. But naturally this is hard work. The man's character, as it stands now, is the result of his own previous actions and thoughts. You who are familiar with the idea of reincarnation, with the thought that this life is only one day in the far larger life, will recognize that this day must depend upon all other days, and that the man is now what he has made himself by antecedent development. But he has lived through many lives, and that means that he has been many thousands of years in training himself to be what he is, even though such training has been unconscious on his part and without any definite aim. He has therefore established within himself many decided habits. We all know how difficult it is to conquer habit — how almost impossible it is to get rid of even some small physical trick of manner when once it has become a part of ourselves. Reasoning from small things to larger ones, we may readily realize that when a man has certain habits which have been steadily strengthening themselves for thousands of years, it is a serious task for him to try to check their momentum and to reverse the currents. These lines of thought and feeling are welded into the man, and they show as qualities which seem to be deeply ingrained in him. Now that he has yielded to them through all that length of time it seems from the worldly point of view impossible for him to resist them, yet it is by no means impossible from the point of view of the occultists.

If, for example, the man has what we call an irritable character, that is because he has yielded himself to feelings of that nature in previous lives — because he has not developed within himself the virtue of self-control If a man has a narrow, mean, and grasping character, it is because he has not learnt the opposite virtues of generosity and unselfishness. So it is all the way through; the man of open mind and genial heart has built into himself these virtues during the ages that have passed over his head. We are exactly what we have made ourselves. Yet we have become what we are without any special effort of thought or of intention. In those lives that are past we have grown without setting any definite object before us, and we have allowed ourselves to be to a great extent the creatures of our surroundings and circumstances.

In some cases we may have intentionally formed ourselves upon the model of someone whom we admired, and that person may have influenced our lives largely for a time. But obviously this hero of ours, whom we have copied, may have had bad qualities as well as good ones; and at these earlier stages it is little likely that we had the discrimination to choose only the good and to refuse the evil. So we may probably have reproduced in ourselves his undesirable qualities as well as those which were worthy of imitation. You may see that this is so if you watch the actions of children in the present day, for from them we may learn much as to the probable actions of the child-nature of our undeveloped souls in the past. You may see how sometimes a boy conceives a violent hero-worship for some older person, and tries to model himself upon him. Suppose, for example, that the object of his adoration is some old sailor who can tell him wonderful stories of adventure on stormy seas and in far distant lands. What the boy admires is the courage and endurance of the man, and he respects him for the experience and the knowledge which he has acquired in his wanderings. He cannot immediately reproduce the courage, the endurance, or the experience; but he can, and he does forthwith, copy the outward traits of his sailor-friend, and so he will faithfully imitate the curious nautical expressions, the tobacco-chewing and the rolling gait. Much in the same way we also may have been hero-worshippers in days and lives gone by, and we may have set up many an unpleasant habit in mimicry of some savage chieftain whose boastful bravery extorted our admiration.

It is probable, however, that this idea (of definitely taking ourselves in hand for the sake of improvement) has occurred to few of us before this life. There is no question that to uproot old bad habits and to replace them by good ones means a great deal of trouble and a great deal of arduous self-control. It is a serious task, and the ordinary man has no knowledge of any motive sufficiently powerful to induce him to attempt it. In the absence of this adequate motive, he does not see why he should put himself to so much and such serious trouble. He probably thinks of himself as a good fellow on the whole, though possibly with one or two amiable weaknesses; but he reflects that everyone has his weaknesses, and that those of many other people are much worse than any which he observes in himself. So he lets himself drift along without making any effort.

Before such a man can be expected to reverse his old habits, and set to work painfully to form new ones, he must first realize the necessity of a change of standpoint, and must obtain a wider view of life as a whole. The ordinary man of the world is frankly, cynically selfish. I do not mean that he is intentionally cruel, or that he is devoid of good feelings; on the contrary, he may often have good and generous impulses. But his life on the whole is certainly a self-centred life; his own personality is the pivot round which the majority of his thought revolves; he judges everything instantly and instinctively by the way in which it happens to affect him personally. Either he is absorbed in the pursuit of wealth, and blind to the higher side of things and to the spiritual life, or else his chief object in existence appears to be the physical enjoyment of the moment.

THE AVERAGE IRRESPONSIBLE FACULTY

To see that this is so, we have only to look round us at the men whom we meet every day, or to listen to the conversations which are going on in the streets or the railway carriages. In nine cases out of ten we shall notice that the people are talking either about money, or amusements, or gossip. Their one idea in life seems to be what they call "having a good time", or, as they frequently put it in still coarser and more objectionable language, "having lots of fun" — as though this were the end and the object of the existence of a reasonable being, a living spark made in the Divine Image! I have been much struck with this — that the only idea which many people seem to connect with life is that of the sensuous pleasure of the moment — just amusement and nothing else. That seems to be all that they are able to comprehend, and it appears to be a sufficient reason for not having visited a certain place to say that there is no "fun" to be had there. I have often heard a similar remark made in France; there also s'amuser bien seems to be the great duty which is recognized by the majority, and it has passed into a figure of ordinary speech, so that a man will often write to another, "I hope you are amusing yourself well" — as though the pleasure of the moment were the only important business.

To listen to the conversation of these men and women of the present age one would suppose them to be the mere insects of a day, with no sense of duty, of responsibility, or of seriousness; they have not in the least realized themselves as immortal souls who are here for a purpose, and have a definite evolution before them; and so their life is one of shallow ignorance and giggling vacuity. The only life they seem to know is the life of the moment, and in this way they lower themselves to the level of the least intelligent of the animals about them. Man has been defined as a thinking animal, but it seems evident that as yet that definition applies only to part of the race. I think we must admit that to one or other of these two classes — the money-hunters, or the pleasure-hunters — belong the majority of the people of our occidental races, and that those whose principal thoughts in life are duty and the pursuit of spiritual development are only a small minority.

There are many of them who have a recognition of duty in connection with their business, and they consider that everything else must yield to that — even their personal pleasure. You will hear a man say, "I should like to do this, but I have my business which requires attention; I cannot afford to lose time from my business". So that even the idea of personal pleasure becomes subsidiary to that of business. This is at least somewhat of an improvement, though it is often sadly overdone, and you will find many people to whom this idea of business has in its turn become a kind of god which they worship. They are in a condition of abject slavery to it, and they never can let themselves escape from its influence even for a moment. They bring it home with them, they are wholly involved with it, and they even dream of it at night; so that they sacrifice everything to this Moloch of business, and they cannot be said to have time for any true life at all. It will be seen that though there is here a dawning conception of duty it is still only upon the physical plane, and their thought is still limited to the affairs of the day. Only in the case of a small number will it be found that this idea is dominated by a light from higher planes; rarely indeed has the man a glimpse of wider horizon. This concentration of attention upon the physical life of the passing day seems to be a characteristic of our present race, of the great so-called civilization which at present exists both in Europe and in America. Obviously the man who wishes to do anything definite in the way of character-building must first of all change this standpoint, for otherwise he has no adequate motive for undertaking so severe a task.

CONVERSION

In religious circles this change of standpoint is called conversion; and if it were freed from the somewhat unpleasant canting associations with which it is ordinarily surrounded, this would be a good word to express exactly what happens to the man. We know that in Latin verto means "to turn", and con signifies "together with", so conversion is the point at which the man turns from following selfish ends and fighting against the great stream of divine evolution, and henceforth begins to understand his position and to move along with that stream. In the Hindu religion they call this same change by the name of viveka, or "discrimination", because when that comes to a man it means that he has learnt to see the relative value of objects and to distinguish to some extent between the real and the unreal, so that he is able to perceive that the higher things only are those which are worthy of his attention. In the Buddhist religion another name is given to this change — mano-dvaravarjana, or "the opening of the doors of the mind". The man's mind has in reality opened its doors; discrimination has awakened within it and its owner has brought it to bear upon the problems of life. The man who is wrapped up in pleasure has not yet opened his mind at all; he is not thinking about life in any serious way, but is immersed in the lower currents. The business man has developed the desire for acquisition, and is bending all his energies into action for that purpose; but his mind also has not yet opened to understand the realities of a higher life.

This opening of the doors, this discrimination, this conversion, means the realization that the things which are seen upon the physical plane are temporal and of little importance as compared with these other things which are unseen and eternal. It is precisely that which is spoken of in the Bible, when we are told: "Set your affection on things above and not on things of the earth ... for the things which are seen are temporal, but the things which are not seen are eternal". This does not mean that a man must give up his ordinary daily life, or must abandon his business or his duties in order to become what is commonly called a pious or a devout man; but it does mean that he should learn intelligently to appreciate other things besides those which are immediately obvious upon the physical plane.

We all of us at different stages have to learn to do this; we have to learn to widen our horizon. As little children, for example, we appreciate only those things which are near to us, and we are unable to look far ahead in time, or to plan much for the future. But as we grow older we learn by experience that it is sometimes necessary for us to give up the pleasures of the moment in order that we may gain something in the future which shall be better and greater. In the first place this is usually to gain something still for ourselves; for it is only by degrees that the true unselfishness dawns. In many cases the little child would spend the whole of his time in play if he were allowed to do so, and it is a matter of regret to him that restrictions are imposed upon him and that he is compelled to learn. Yet we universally recognize that the child should learn, because we know what the child as yet does not — that that learning will fit him to take his place in life, and to have a fuller and more useful career than would be possible for him if instead of learning he devoted himself entirely to the joys of the moment.

Yet we who thus enforce this learning upon the child are ourselves doing the same thing for which we blame the little one, when we regard the matter from a somewhat higher standpoint. We also are working for the moment — for the moment of this one life, and we fail to realize that there is something infinitely grander and higher and happier within reach if we only understood it. We are working for this one day only, and not for the future which will be eternal. The moment a man becomes convinced of this higher life and of the eternal future — as soon as he realizes that he has his part to play in that, naturally his common sense asserts itself, and he says to himself: "If that be so, obviously these material things are of comparatively little account, and instead of wasting the whole of my time I must be learning to prepare myself for this greater life in the future. There at once is the adequate motive whose lack we previously deplored; there is the incentive to learn to build the character, in order to fit oneself for that other and higher life.

PURITANISM

I think that Puritanism, which has played such a prominent part in the history both of England and of America, arose chiefly as a reaction against that view of life of which I was speaking just now — the mere living for the careless selfish enjoyment of the moment. I believe that Puritanism was in itself largely a protest against that, and in so far as it emphasizes the reality of the higher life, and the necessity of paying attention to it, it had good in it. True, it also did much harm — more harm than good on the whole, because it did this terrible thing, that it made people identify religion with sourness and sadness. It made people think that to be good one must be miserable; it degraded and all but destroyed the idea of the loving Father. It blasphemed God by telling horrible and wicked falsehoods with regard to Him; it misrepresented Him as a stern and cruel judge, a monster, instead of a Father full of love and compassion; and in doing this it warped and distorted Anglo-Saxon Christianity, and set a stamp upon it from which it has not even yet recovered.

Perhaps the reason of this may be that it made a common mistake — that it confused cause and effect. It is true that a man who has learned to appreciate the higher joys of the spiritual life cares little for those of the ordinary physical existence. That is not because he has lost his capacity for joy, but because he has now realized something so much fuller and wider, that by comparison with it the lower delight has ceased to seem joy at all. When the boy comes to be a man he has outgrown his childish toys, yet he is capable of other and much greater pleasures than those could ever have given him. Just so the man who rises in evolution, so that instead of mere selfish delights he comes to appreciate the far greater joy of unselfish work, will find that his ordinary pleasures are no longer satisfying to him and seem to him no longer worth the trouble of pursuit. This is because he has reached a higher standpoint and gained a wider horizon; but the result upon the physical plane gives the impression that he has ceased to be interested in the lower physical pleasures.

We must not, however, confuse the cause with the effect as the unfortunate Puritans did, and suppose that by turning our backs upon the joys of the physical plane we therefore instantly become the more highly evolved men with the wider outlook. It is true that because the young man has developed he no longer cares for infantile pleasures; it would not be true that the infant by refusing the delights appropriate to his age would thereby become an adult. It is well, then, that we should realize clearly that it is emphatically a false and foolish doctrine that to be good men must be miserable. Exactly; the reverse is the truth, for God means man to be happy, and it is certainly his duty to be so; for a man who is unhappy radiates depression all round him, and thus makes life harder for his fellow men.

How then does a man come to make this great effort of trying to build his character, trying to make something of himself? The safest and the most satisfactory path is that which we have just indicated. The man comes to wider knowledge, he comes to understand that there is a grander and higher life; he sees that there is a great scheme, and that man is part of that scheme. Seeing that, and appreciating to some extent the splendour and the glory of the plan, he wishes to become an intelligent part of it — he wishes to take his place in it, no longer merely as a straw swept along by a storm, but rather as one who understands and desires to take his share in the mighty divine work that is being done.

There are others whose awakening comes along a different line — the line of devotion, rather than of knowledge. They are strongly attracted either by a high ideal or by some lofty personality; their love and admiration are excited, and for the sake of that ideal, for the sake of that personality, they make strenuous endeavours to develop themselves. When this devotion is inspired by the glimpse of a splendid ideal it is indeed a glorious thing, and its action is practically indistinguishable from that of spiritual knowledge. When the devotion is to a person it is often hardly less beautiful, though then there is a certain element of danger arising from the fact that the object of this intense affection is human and must therefore possess imperfections. Sometimes it happens that the devotee comes suddenly upon one of these imperfections, and receives therefrom a rude shock which may tend to diminish or divert the devotion. The high ideal can never fail the man who trusts it; the person may always do so to some extent or in some respect, and consequently there is less security in the devotion to a teacher.

We in The Theosophical Society have had some experience in this direction, for among our students there are many who approach the truth by this road of devotion. When the devotion is to Theosophy, all goes well; their enthusiasm grows ever more and more brilliant as they learn more of the truth; and no matter how far they penetrate, or which of its many sides they investigate, they can never be disappointed. But when the devotion has been not to Theosophy or to the great Masters who gave it to the world, but to some one of their instruments on the physical plane, we have found that its basis is less secure. Many entered the Society and took up its studies on the strength of a personal devotion to its great founder, Madame Blavatsky. Those who knew her most intimately, those who came nearest to understanding that wonderful many-sided individuality, never lost their faith in her, nor their deep heartfelt affection and devotion for her; but others who knew less of her were perturbed when they read or heard of wild accusations brought against her, or when they saw the unfavourable report of a learned Society concerning her. Then it often happened that because their faith had been based upon the personality (and upon one which they did not understand) they found themselves altogether overthrown, and abandoned the study of Theosophy for this incarnation. Such action is obviously utterly irrational, for even if all the absurd stories circulated about Madame Blavatsky had been true, the mighty doctrines of Theosophy still remain the same, and its system is still unassailable; but the emotional person does not reason, and so when the prejudices of these good people were shocked or their feelings were hurt, they abandoned the Society in a rage, not realizing that they were themselves the only sufferers through their folly.

Devotion is a splendid force; yet without an intelligent comprehension of that to which the devotion is felt, it has often led people terribly wrong. But if the man clearly grasps the mighty divine scheme of evolution, and feels his devotion called forth by that, then all is well with him, for that cannot fail him, and the more he knows of it the deeper his devotion will become and the more thoroughly will he identify himself with it. There is no fear of close investigation there, for fuller knowledge means deeper adoration, greater wonder, profounder love. For these reasons it is best for the man to feel his devotion for the ideals rather than for personalities, however lofty these may be. Best of all is it that he should base himself upon reason and fact, and argue from what is well known scientifically to the things not yet known in the outer world. His inferences may sometimes be wrong, but he realizes that possibility, and is always ready to change them if good reason can be shown to him. Any such alterations in detail cannot affect the basis upon which his system rests, since that is not accepted upon blind faith, but stands on the secure platform of reason and of common sense. He knows that the mighty scheme of evolution exists, although as yet our knowledge of it is imperfect; he knows that he is put here for a purpose, and that he ought to be trying to do his share in the work of the world. How then can he begin to fit himself to take that share ?

There comes in the question of the building of character. A man sees himself to be fit or unfit as the case may be; to be fit in certain ways perhaps, but much hampered in others by characteristics which he possesses. There at once is an adequate motive for him to take himself in hand, when he realizes that his life is not for this short and fleeting period only, but for all eternity, when he sees that the conditions of the future days of this wider life will be modified by his actions now. He recognizes that he must so train himself as to be able to do this noble work which he sees opening up before him — that he must not waste his time in idleness or folly, because if he does he cannot sustain the part destined for him. He must learn, he must educate and develop himself in various ways in order that he may not fail in his ability to bear his share in the future that awaits us, in the glory that shall be revealed.

As to the stages in which this can be done, perhaps, we can hardly do better than listen to the words of one of the mightiest of the earth's Teachers. You will remember that men asked the Lord Buddha to state the whole of his marvellous doctrine in one single verse; and that he replied in these memorable words: "Cease to do evil; learn to do well; cleanse your own heart; this is the teaching of the Buddhas". Let us take up the building of character along the lines indicated by the golden words of the great Indian Prince, and see how thoroughly his single sentence covers the work of many lives.

"Cease to do evil."Let us look at ourselves carefully and thoughtfully, examine ourselves and see what there is in us that stands in our way, that prevents us from being perfect characters. We know the goal that is set before us; we who have read the Theosophical books know what is written there of the great Masters of Wisdom — of those men who are almost more than men, and of their glory, power, compassion, and wisdom. There is no mystery as to the qualifications of the adept; the steps of the path of holiness are fully described in our books, with the qualities which belong to each of them.

What the Masters are, what the Buddha was, what the Christ was, that we must all some day become; we may therefore set before ourselves what is known of these exalted characters, and putting ourselves in comparison with them we shall see at once in how many ways we fall lamentably short of that grand ideal. Lamentably, yet not hopelessly, for these great Masters assure us that they have risen from the ranks in which we are now toiling, and that as they are now so we shall be in the future; and whether that future be near or distant is a matter which is entirely in our own hands, and rests upon our own exertions.

The attempt to compare ourselves with these perfect men will at once reveal to us the existence of many faults and failings in ourselves which have long ago disappeared from them. Thus we commence our effort to obey the command of the Buddha, "Cease to do evil", by setting to work to eradicate these undesirable qualities. We have not far to look for them. Let us take, for example, the quality of irritability — a very common failing in a civilization such as ours, in which there is such a constant rush and whirl, and so much of nervous overstrain. Here is a prominent evil which must certainly be cast out. A man often thinks of himself as having been born with a highly-strung nervous organism, and therefore unable to help feeling things more keenly than other people; and so he expresses this additional sensitiveness by irritability. That is the mistake which he makes. It may be true that he is keenly sensitive; as the race develops many people are becoming so. Yet the fact remains that the man himself should remain master of his vehicles and not allow himself to be swept away by the storm of passion.

ASTRAL DISTURBANCE

This irritability is seen by the clairvoyant as liability to disturbance in the astral body. This astral body is a vehicle with which the man has clothed himself in order that he may learn through it and act through it. It cannot therefore fulfil its purpose unless he has it thoroughly under control. As the Indian books tell us, these passions and desires are like horses — in order to be useful to us they must be under the control of the mind who is the driver; and this driver himself must also be ready to obey the slightest order which comes from the true man who sits in the chariot directing the movement of these his servants. For the man to allow himself to be swayed or swept from his base by his passions and emotions, is to allow his horses to run away with him and to carry him whither they will instead of whither he will. It is for us to say whether we will allow ourselves to be mastered in this undignified manner by these feelings which should be our servants. We have the right and the power to say that this shall not be, and that these unruly horses shall be brought under control. It may be true that for a long time we have allowed them to have their own way until to yield to them instead of dominating them has become a fixed habit. Yet to learn to manage them is the first step in the upward path; there can be no question that it will have to be taken, and the sooner it is taken the easier it will be.

It can never be too late to begin, and it is obvious that each time that the man yields himself makes it a little more difficult for him to resume the control later. The irritable man constantly finds himself succumbing to small annoyances, and under their influence saying and doing what afterwards he bitterly regrets. Strong though his resolve may be, again and again the old habit asserts itself, and he finds that he has said or done something under its influence before (as he would put it) he has had time to think. Still if he continues to make a determined effort at control, he will eventually reach a stage when he is able to check himself in the very utterance of a hasty word, and to turn aside the current of his annoyance when it is at its strongest. From that to the stage where he will check himself before he utters that word is not a long step, and when that has been gained he is near the final victory. Then he has conquered the outward expression of the feeling of irritation; and after that he will not find it difficult to avoid the feeling altogether. When that has been once done a definite step has been gained, for the quality of irritability has been weeded out, and it has been replaced by the quality of patience as a permanent possession, which the man will carry on with him into all his future births.

CONCEIT AND PREJUDICE

Men have many failings which they hardly notice, yet if they carefully examine and judge themselves by sufficiently high standards they cannot help perceiving where they fall short. One of the commonest of all failings is self-conceit. It is so natural for a man to wish to think well of himself, to emphasize in his mind those points in which he considers he excels, and to attach undue importance to them, and at the same time to slur over almost without thought the many other points in which he falls short of other men. This self-conceit is a quality which needs to be carefully watched and steadily suppressed whenever it shows its head, for it is not only one of the commonest of all, but it is one of the most difficult to master; when conquered in one direction it reappears under some new guise in another. It is subtle and far-reaching, and it disguises itself with great success; yet until it is eradicated but little progress is possible.

Another weed which must be relentlessly torn up is prejudice. So often we are exceedingly intolerant of any new idea, of any other belief than our own; we are set and firm and dogmatic along certain lines, and unwilling to listen to truth. For example, we have our prejudices as to what we call morality, based exclusively upon conventional ideas; any suggestion which contravenes these, no matter how reasonable it may be, gives us such a shock that we lose our heads altogether, and become rabid and full of hatred, bitter and persecuting in our opposition to it. Many a man who thinks himself free from intolerance because he has no special religious belief is just as dogmatic along his own materialistic lines as the worst religious fanatic could be. Often a scientific man regards religion of all kinds with easy tolerance, considering it as something only fit for women and children. He looks down with amused superiority upon the horror with which one religious sect regards the opinions of another, and wonders why they should make so much fuss about a matter which can hardly be of serious importance one way or the other; and yet at the same time he has certain fixed ideas with regard to science, about which he is just as bigoted as are his religious friends in their dogmas. It does not occur to him that there is a bigotry outside of religion, and that in science, as well as in faith, a man's mind must always remain open to the advent of new truth, even though that truth may overthrow many of his own preconceived ideas.

Often this vice or prejudice is a subtle manifestation of that self-conceit to which I previously referred; the set of ideas which the man has adopted are his ideas and for that reason they must be treated with respect, and anything which tends to conflict with them cannot be entertained for a moment, because to receive it would be to admit that he may have been mistaken. Many a man has within him pettinesses, meanness, narrowness of mind, the existence of which he has not suspected; yet these qualities will manifest themselves when circumstances arise which call them into action.

Often, even when a man sees the manifestation of some such undesirable quality within himself, he to some extent excuses it by saying that it is after all natural. But what do we mean by this word natural ? Simply that the majority of mankind would be likely under similar circumstances to display such a quality, and so the man in whom it manifests is an average man. Yet we should remember that if we are trying to take ourselves in hand and to build our character towards the high ideal which we have set before us, we are aiming to raise ourselves above the average man, so that what is natural for him will not be sufficient in the higher life which we are now endeavouring to live. We must rise above that which is natural for the average of the race, and we must bring ourselves into a condition in which only that which is right and good and true shall be the natural course for us. We must eradicate the evil, and replace it by good, so that it is the expression of the latter which will instinctively show itself when we act without premeditation. If we are trying to realize the higher life, trying to make ourselves a channel through which the divine force may pour out upon our fellow men, then that which is natural as yet for the majority will be unworthy of our higher aspirations. Therefore we must not excuse faults and failings in ourselves because they are natural, but we must set to work to make that natural to us which we desire to have within us; and this development also is entirely within our own hands.

KUSALASSA UPASAMPADA

Sometimes the easiest way to carry out the first command "Cease to do evil" is to commence by trying to obey the second one "Learn to do well". If we wish to conquer an evil habit, it is sometimes easier and better for us to make strenuous efforts to develop within ourselves the opposite virtue. What are the qualities which are most necessary for us ? If we can examine the matter without prejudice we shall find that very many of those which go to make the perfect man are as yet sadly lacking in us. Take first the very important quality of self-control. The majority of us are certainly deficient in this respect, and this fact shows itself in a dozen ways. The irritability of which I spoke previously is one of the commonest forms in which lack of self-control shows itself. There are other and coarser passions, such as the desire of the drunkard or of the sensualist, which most of us have already learned to control, or perhaps we have eliminated them from our natures in previous lives. But if any relics of such coarser passions still remain with us in the form of gluttony or sensuality, our first step must be to bring such desires under the dominion of the will.

In such cases as this the necessity is obvious to everyone; but our lack of self-control may show itself in other ways which we do not so readily perceive. When some trouble, some sorrow or suffering comes to a man, he often allows himself to be greatly worried or profoundly depressed by it. Instead of maintaining his attitude of calmness and serenity, he identifies himself with the lower vehicle, and allows himself to be swept away. He must learn to take a firm stand — to say to himself: "These forces from without are playing upon my lower vehicles, affecting perhaps my physical body or my astral body, but I, the Soul, the true Man, stand above all these things; I remain untroubled, and I will not allow myself to be disturbed or moved by them."

THE FOOLISHNESS OF TAKING OFFENCE

Another instance which is painfully common is the way in which a man takes offence at something which another says or does. If you think of it this also shows a strange lack, not only of self-control, but of common sense. What the other man says or does cannot make any difference to you. If he has said something that has hurt your feelings, you may be sure that in nine cases out of ten he has not meant it to be offensive; why then should you allow yourself to be disturbed about the matter ? Even in the rare cases where a, remark is intentionally rude or spiteful — where a man has said something purposely to wound another — how foolish it is for that other to allow himself to feel hurt! If the man had an evil intention in what he said, he is much to be pitied, since we know that under the law of divine justice he will certainly suffer for his foolishness. What he has said need in no way affect you; if a man strikes a blow on the physical plane, it is no doubt desirable for you to defend yourself against its repetition, because there is a definite injury; but in the case of the irritating word no effect whatever is really produced. A blow which strikes your physical body is a perceptible impact from outside; the irritating word does not in any way injure you, except in so far as you may choose to take it up and injure yourself by brooding over it or allowing yourself to be wounded in your feelings. What are the words of another, that you should let your serenity be disturbed by them? They are merely a vibration in the atmosphere; if it had not happened that you heard them, or heard of them, would they have affected you ? If not, then it is obviously not the words that have injured you, but the fact that you heard them. So if you allow yourself to care about what a man has said, it is you who are responsible for the disturbance created in your astral body, and not he. The man has done and can do nothing that can harm you; if you feel hurt and injured and thereby make yourself a great deal of trouble, you have only yourself to thank for it. If a disturbance arises within your astral body in reference to what he has said, that is merely because you have not yet gained control over that body; you have not yet developed the calmness which enables you to look down as a soul upon all this and go on your way and attend to your own work without taking the slightest notice of foolish or spiteful remarks made by other men.

If you will attain this calmness and serenity, you will find that your life is infinitely happier than before. I do not put that before you as the reason for which you should seek this development; it is a good reason truly, yet there is another and higher reason in the fact that we have work to do for our fellow men and that we cannot be fit to do it unless we are calm and serene. It is always best that we should keep before ourselves this highest of all reasons for self-development — that unless we evolve ourselves we cannot be a fit and perfect channel for the divine power and strength. That should be our motive in our effort; yet the fact remains that the result of this effort will be greatly increased happiness in our work. The man who cultivates calmness and serenity soon finds the joyousness of the divine life pervading the whole of his existence. To the clairvoyant who can observe the higher bodies the change in such a man is remarkable and beautiful to see.

THE EVIL OF UNNECESSARY AGITATION

The average man is usually a centre of agitated vibration; he is constantly in a condition of worry or trouble about something, or in a condition of deep depression, or else he is unduly excited in the endeavour to grasp something. For one reason or another he is always in a state of unnecessary agitation, generally about the merest trifle. Although he never thinks of it, he is all the while influencing other people around him by this condition of his astral body. He is communicating these vibrations and this agitation to the unfortunate people who are near him; and it is just because millions of people are thus unnecessarily agitated by all sorts of foolish desires and feelings that it is so difficult for the sensitive person to live in a great city or to go into any large crowd of his fellow men. An examination of the illustration of the effect of the various emotions as shown in Man Visible and Invisible will at once enable us to realize that a man in such a condition of agitation must be causing great disturbance in the astral world about him, and we shall see that others who happen to be in his neighbourhood cannot remain unaffected by the influence which pours out from him. The man who gives way to passion is sending out waves of passion; the man who allows himself to fall into a condition of deep depression is radiating in all directions waves of depression; so that each of these men is making life harder for all those who are so unfortunate as to be near him.

In modern life every man has little circumstances which worry him, which tend to stir up irritability within him; every man has sooner or later some cause for worry and for depression; and whenever any one of us yields to either of these feelings the vibrations which we send out assuredly tend to accentuate the difficulties of all our neighbours. Such vibrations make it harder for those about us to resist the next accession of irritability or depression which may come to them; if there are germs of these qualities in them, the vibrations which we have so wrongly allowed ourselves to send forth may awaken these germs when otherwise they would have lain dormant. No man has a right to commit this crime of throwing obstacles in the way of his fellow men; no man has a right to yield himself to depression or to give way to anger — not only because these things are evil for him and wrong in themselves, but because they do harm to those around him.

On the other hand, if we cultivate within ourselves serenity, calmness, and joyousness, we make life lighter instead of darker for all those into whose presence we come; we spread about us soothing vibrations, we make it easier for our neighbours to resist worry or trouble or annoyance, and thus we help to lift the burdens from all those who are about us, although we may say never a word to them! Every one is the better because we are calm and strong, because we have realized the duty of the soul. Here, then, are some useful qualities which we may seek to build into ourselves — the qualities of self-control, happiness, and calmness. Let us learn that it is our duty to be happy, because God means man to be happy. Therefore it is that the man must not let himself be swept off his feet by the waves of thought and feeling about him, but must stand firm as a tower to which others may cling who are still affected by these waves. So shall divine strength flow through him to those others, and they too shall be rescued from the stormy ocean of life, and brought into the haven where they would be.

COURAGE AND RESOLUTION

Other virtues which we should build into ourselves are courage and determination. There are many men in the world who have an iron determination within them about certain things — a resolution that nothing can shake. They have resolved to make money, and they will do it — honestly, if possible, but at any rate they will make it; and these men usually succeed to a greater or less extent. We who are students of a higher life think of them as narrow in their outlook, as understanding but little of what life really is. That is true, yet we should remember that they are at least living up in practice to what they understand. The one thing of which they feel certain is that money is a great good, and that they intend to have plenty of it; and they are throwing their whole strength into that effort. We have convinced ourselves that there is something higher in the world than the gaining of money, that there is a vaster and a grander life, the smallest glimpse of which is worth more than all mere earthly gain. If we are as thoroughly convinced of the beauty of the higher life as is the worldly man of the desirability of making money, we shall throw ourselves into the pursuit of that higher life with exactly the same resolution and enthusiasm with which he throws himself into the pursuit of gold. He neglects no possibility, he will take infinite pains to qualify himself to pursue his object better; may not we often learn a lesson from him as to the one-pointedness and the untiring energy with which he devotes himself to his object ? True, the object itself is an illusion, and when he gains it he often finds it to be of but little value after all; yet the qualities which he has developed in that struggle cannot but be valuable to him when the higher light dawns upon him and he is able to turn his talents to a better use.

In this development of resolution the study of Theosophy greatly helps us. The Theosophist realizes profoundly the infinity of work in the direction of self-development which lies before him; yet he can never be depressed, as the wordly man sometimes is, by the feeling that he is now growing old, that his time is short, and that he cannot hope to attain his end before death puts a period to his effort. The student of occultism recognizes that he has eternity before him for his work, and that in that eternity he can make himself exactly what he desires to be. There is nothing that can prevent him. He finds around him many limitations which he has made for himself in previous lives; yet with eternity before him all these limitations will be transcended, his end will be accomplished, his goal will be attained.

There are many people who are anxious to know what the future has in store for them — so many that large numbers of swindlers live upon this desire. Any astrologer or clairvoyant who thinks he can predict the future is certain to have immense numbers of clients; even the veriest charlatan seems to be able to make a living by a mere pretence to the occult arts or to prevision. Yet in truth no one need trouble himself in the slightest degree about his future, for it will be exactly what he intends that it shall be. The student of occultism does not seek to know what the future has in store for him; he says rather: "I intend to do this or that; I know what my future development will be, because I know what I intend to make it. There may be many obstacles in my way, put there by my own previous actions; I do not know how many there are, or in what form they may come; I do not even care to know. Whatever they may be, my resolution is unshaken; whether it be in this life or in future lives, I shall mould my existence as I like; and in knowing that, I know all that I care to know of that which lies before me." When the man realizes the divine power which resides within him he cares little for outward circumstances; he decides upon what he will do; he devotes his energy to it and he carries it through; he says to himself: "This shall be done; how long it will take matters nothing, but I will do it." It will be seen therefore that courage and determination are virtues which are emphatically necessary for the student of occultism.

THE GREATEST NEED OF ALL

Most of all man needs to develop the quality of unselfishness; for man as we find him at present is by nature terribly selfish. In saying that, we are not casting blame upon him for his past; we are trying to remind him that there lies before him a future. The Theosophist understands why this fault of selfishness should be so common among men, for he realizes what has been the birth and the growth of the soul in man. He knows that the individual was slowly, gradually formed through ages of evolution, and consequently that the individuality is very strongly marked in man. The soul as a centre of strength has grown up within the walls of self, and without these protecting walls the man could not have been what he now is. But now he has reached the stage where the powerful centre is definitely established, and consequently he has to break down this scaffolding of selfish thought which surrounds him. This shell was a necessity, no doubt, for the formation of the centre; but now that the centre is formed the shell must be broken away, because while it exists it prevents the centre from doing its duty, and from carrying out the work for which it was formed. The man has become a sun, from which the divine power should radiate upon all those around him, and this radiation cannot be until the walls of selfishness have been broken down.

It is not wonderful that it should be hard for man to do this, for in getting rid of selfishness he is conquering a habit which he has spent many ages in forming. It had its use and its place in these earlier stages; as one of the Masters of Wisdom once put it: "The law of the survival of the fittest is the law of evolution for the brute; but the law of intelligent self-sacrifice is the law of development for man." So it comes that man needs to transcend what was formerly his nature and to build into himself the quality of unselfishness, the quality of love, so that he may learn gladly to sacrifice what seems his personal interest for the good of humanity as a whole.

Let us beware that we do not misunderstand this. I do not mean by that any development of cheap sentimentalism. Men who are new to this study sometimes think that it is expected of them that they shall attain to the level of loving all their brethren alike. That is an impossibility even if it were desirable; and to see that this is so we have only to turn to the example of the highest of men. Remember that it is related of Jesus himself that he had his beloved disciple St. John, and of the Buddha that he was more closely attached to the disciple Ananda than to many others who possessed greater powers and higher advancement. It is not demanded of us, it is not intended, that we should have the same feeling of affection towards all. It is true that such affection as we now feel towards those who are nearest and dearest to us, we shall presently come to feel for all our brother-men; but when that time comes our affection for those whom we love best will have become something infinitely greater than it is now. It will mean that our power of affection has grown enormously, but not that it has ceased to be stronger in one case than it is in another — not that all the world has become the same to us,

What is important for us now is that we should regard all mankind, not with hostility, but in that friendly attitude which is watching for an opportunity to serve. When we feel deep affection or gratitude towards some person we watch constantly for an opportunity to do some little thing for him to show our gratitude, our respect, our affection, or our reverence. Let us adopt that attitude of ready helpfulness towards all mankind; let us be always prepared to do whatever comes to our hand — ever watching for an opportunity to serve our fellow men, and let us regard every contact with another man as an opportunity of being useful to him in some way or other. In that way we shall learn to build into our character these important virtues of love and unselfishness.

SINGLE-MINDEDNESS

Another necessary quality is that of single-mindedness. We must learn that the great object of our lives is to make ourselves a channel for the divine force, and that that object therefore must always be the determining factor in any decision that we make. When two paths open before us, instead of stopping to consider which of these two would be best for us individually, we must learn to think rather which is the noblest, which is the most useful, which will bring most good to other men. When in business or in social life we take some step which appears advantageous for us we should ask ourselves in all sincerity, "Can this thing, which seems as though it would bring good to me, do some harm to someone else ? Am I making an apparent gain at the cost of a loss to some other man ? If that be so I will have none of it; I will not enter upon any such course of action. For that cannot be right for me which brings harm to my brothers; I must never raise myself by trampling down others." Thus we must learn in everything to make the highest our criterion, and steadily little by little to build these virtues into ourselves. The process may be a slow one, but the result is sure.

SACHITTA PARIYODAPANAM

Nor must we forget the third line of the Buddha's verse: "Cleanse your own heart". Begin with your thoughts; keep them high and unselfish, and your actions will follow along the same line. What is required is intelligent adaptation to the conditions of the true life. Here on the physical plane we have to live in accordance with the laws of the plane. For example, there are certain laws of hygiene, and the intelligent man adapts himself carefully to them, knowing that if he does not his life will be an imperfect one and full of physical suffering. Every cultured man knows that to be the merest common sense; yet we see daily how difficult it is to induce the ignorant and uneducated to comply with these natural laws. We who have learnt them adapt ourselves to them as a matter of course, and we realize that if we did not do so we should be acting foolishly, and if we suffered from such action we should have only ourselves to blame.

We who are students of occultism have through our studies learnt much of the conditions of a higher and grander life. We have learnt that just as there are certain physical laws which must be obeyed if the physical life is to be lived healthily and happily, so there are the moral laws of this higher and wider life, which it is also necessary to obey if we wish to make that life happy and useful. Having learnt these Jaws, we must use intelligence and common sense in living according to them. It is with a view of adapting ourselves to them that we watch, ourselves with reference to these qualities of which we have spoken. The wise man takes them one at a time, and examines himself carefully with reference to the quality which he has chosen, to see where he is lacking in it. He thinks beforehand of opportunities for displaying that quality, yet he is always ready to take other unexpected opportunities when he finds them opening up before him. He keeps that quality, as it were, in the back of his mind always, and tries perseveringly from day to day, and every moment of the day, to live up to his highest conception of it. If he thus keeps it steadily before him, he will soon find a great change coming over him; and when he feels that he has thoroughly grounded himself in that, so that its practice has become a habit and a matter of instinct with him, he takes up another quality and works in the same way with that.

NO MORBID INTROSPECTION

That is the method of procedure, yet we must be careful in adopting it not to fall into a common error. We may remember that the Buddha advises his disciples to follow the middle path in everything, warning them that extremes in either direction are invariably dangerous. That is true in this case also. The ordinary man of the world is asleep in regard to the whole of this question of the cultivation of character; its necessity has never dawned above his horizon, and he is blankly ignorant with regard to it. That is one extreme, and the worst of all. The other extreme is to be found in the constant morbid introspection in which some of the best people indulge. They are so constantly mourning over their faults and failings that they have no time to be useful to their fellow men; and so they cause themselves unnecessary sorrow and waste much strength and effort while making but little real progress. A little child who has a piece of garden for himself is sometimes so eager to see how his seeds are growing that he digs them up before they have really started in order to examine them again, and so effectually prevents them from springing at all. Some good people seem to be just as impatient as is such a child; they are constantly pulling themselves up by the roots to see how they are growing spiritually, and in this way they hinder all real advancement.

Self-examination and self-knowledge are necessary; but morbid introspection is above all things to be avoided. Often it has its root in a subtle form of self-conceit — an exaggerated opinion of one's importance. A man should set his face in the right direction; he should note his faults and failings, and strive to get rid of them; he should note the good qualities in which he is lacking, and endeavour to develop them within himself. But when he has formed this firm resolve, and in doing his best to carry it into effect, he can well afford to forget himself for the time in the service of his fellow men. If he will but throw himself into earnest unselfish work, in the very act of doing that work he will develop many useful qualities. Having controlled the mind and the senses, let him think often of the highest ideals that he knows; let him think what the Masters are, what the Buddha is, what the Christ is, and let him try to mould his life towards theirs; let him work always with this end in view, and let him try to raise himself towards "the measure of the stature of the fullness of the Christ". Remember that he told us, "Be ye perfect, as your Father in heaven is perfect." Remember also that he would never have uttered those words if it had not been possible for man to fulfil that command. Perfection is possible for us because immortality is a fact; we have all eternity before us in which to work, and yet we have no time to lose; for the sooner we begin to live the life of the Christ, the sooner we shall be in a position to do the work of the Christ, and to range ourselves among the saviours and the helpers of the world.

www.ingramcontent.com/pod-product-compliance
Lightning Source LLC
LaVergne TN
LVHW050946080826
845145LV00004B/1430

* 9 7 8 1 6 3 1 1 8 6 2 6 4 *